·CLOTHING·

Hats, Gloves and Footwear

Helen Whitty
POWERHOUSE MUSEUM

This edition first published in 2002 in the United States of America by Chelsea House Publishers, a subsidiary of Haights Cross Communications

Chelsea House Publishers
1974 Sproul Road, Suite 400
Broomall, PA 19008-0914

The Chelsea House world wide web address is www.chelseahouse.com

Library of Congress Cataloging-in-Publication Data Applied for
ISBN 0-7910-6572-3

First published in 2000 by
Macmillan Education Australia Pty Ltd
627 Chapel Street, South Yarra, Australia, 3141

Unless otherwise indicated, all objects featured in this publication are from the Powerhouse Museum collection. The Museum acknowledges the many generous donations of objects which form a significant part of its collection.

Please visit the Powerhouse Museum at www.phm.gov.au

Curatorial advice: Lindie Ward, Glynis Jones, Peter Cox, Kevin Sumption and Christina Sumner of the Powerhouse Museum
Photography: Powerhouse Museum including Penelope Clay, Marinco Kojdanovski, Sue Stafford
(unless indicated in the picture acknowledgement)
Photo librarian: Kathleen Hackett
Research librarian: Ingrid Mason
Rights and permissions: Gara Baldwin and Judith Matheson
Editorial and production assistance: Judith Matheson
Other assistance: Mandy Crook, Fleur Bishop, Stephanie Boast and Joan Watson
Shoe timeline: Wendy Bishop
Powerhouse Publishing Manager: Julie Donaldson

Edited by Michaela Forster, em rules pty ltd
Text design and page layout by Polar Design Pty Ltd
Cover design by Polar Design Pty Ltd
Illustrations by Wendy Arthur

Printed in Hong Kong

Contents

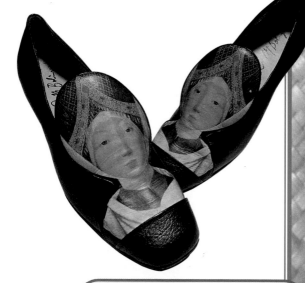

Don't turn this page!
Think of all the things you wear on your head, hands and feet. See if you recognize any of them in this book.

Introduction

The things you wear on your body are your clothes. You probably have things you like to wear and things you have to wear. Your family probably likes you to wear special clothes for certain occasions. Sometimes what you like to wear and what your family wants you to wear are very different. Have you heard someone say, 'I wouldn't be caught dead in that dress/jacket/hat/shoes'? People can feel very strongly about what they, and others, wear.

▼ 'FUNK INC' poster from funkessentials, designed and made in Australia, 1993

The story of clothing is about people's creativity and the ways they like to show it. What people make, wear and care about are examples of this creativity. What people wear says something about them. *Clothing* looks at wearing and making clothes across times, places and cultures.

Don't get dressed up to read this book — just dust off your imagination. Start off by imagining yourself without clothes.

Too revealing? The strange thing is, the more you cover up with clothing, the more you are really saying about yourself.

►

Transparent plastic figure of a woman. It is full size, and shows the body organs, veins and arteries. It was made in 1954 to teach people about health and hygiene.

Hats, gloves and footwear

Hats, gloves and shoes are all the things you can wear on your head, hands and feet. Is this correct? What about **agals**, **aigrettes**, beanies, **balaclavas** and **tiaras** OR mittens, **muffs** and power gloves OR boots, loafers, moccasins, pumps, sneakers and slippers? There are many different things you can wear on these parts of your body. You will see some of them in this book.

▶

'Mary don't ask' wearable sculpture by Peter Tully. Made in Australia in 1984. This outfit has things hung, draped, wrapped and layered all over the body, including the head, hands and feet. Is that headpiece a hat, telephone or tea cup?

Types of hats

There are many different types of hats.
Some of them have special names.

▲ a cap

▲ a crown

◄ an agal

▲
◄ hats
▼

a tiara ►

▲ a Hmong headdress

▲ a balaclava

Hats have always been worn to protect the wearer from the heat or cold, but also as a symbol. Often this symbol is to suggest that the wearer is important. In ancient Greece and Rome, slaves could not wear hats.

a helmet ▶

a fez

▲ a beanie

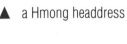

▲ a comb

◀ a cap

an aigrette ▼

a Mandarin hat ▼

◀ a bonnet

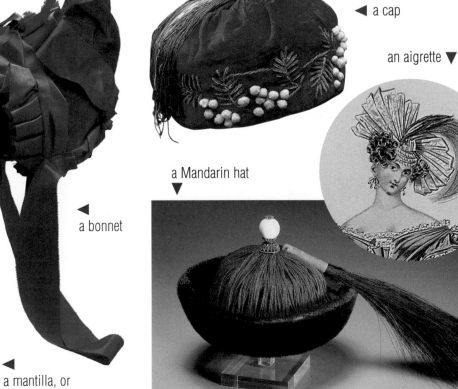

◀ a mantilla, or shawl or scarf

7

Hats made from plants

Hats can be made from materials that are found easily and cheaply, such as plants.

Bamboo

This hat is made of bamboo and gold paper, and is lined with newspaper. It comes from a village on the north coast of Java, Indonesia.

Gourd

This hat is made from a **gourd**, which is like a pumpkin. Inside, it has a woven bamboo shape to fit the head. It was made in the Philippines.

Cabbage-tree hat

Early colonists in Australia wanted hats made of straw like they had in Europe, but straw was not available. Instead, they used **fronds** from the cabbage-tree palm. These were cut into strands and woven to make hats to protect them from the sun.

Coconut

This hat was also made in the Philippines. It is made from coconuts.

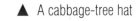

▲ A cabbage-tree hat

'Virtual' hats

The **headset** in this picture makes the wearer feel as if they are in another world—a 'virtual reality'. Virtual reality means 'as if it were real'. You may experience something like this when you play a game with your friends and make up an imaginary world, or when you play games on your computer and see another world on screen. The headset below feeds the wearer's eyes and ears very accurate sounds and pictures from a computer. The screen image is inescapable (unless you take off the headset). This is called an **'immersive** experience'. Whichever way the headset wearer looks, they see a 'view' of the virtual world.

▼ This immersive headset creates a 'virtual reality' for the wearer.

Caps

A cap for a married woman

This cap was made during the 1800s in Eastern Europe. This was a time when you could tell if a woman was married by what she wore on her head. After the wedding ceremony, another ceremony was performed where the wedding head-dress was exchanged for an embroidered cap. It was usually made from hand-spun **linen**, with a hand-embroidered pattern and crochet edging. Married women sang songs and carried candles while circling the new bride. The cap was to protect the woman from bad luck and she was always to wear it.

Unfortunately, the cap and hairstyle which went with it could rub the back of the head bald! These sorts of caps are now only worn at festivals as part of the traditional costume.

What they were wearing then

Sir Douglas Mawson (1882–1958) was a brave and daring Antarctic explorer. He made his first trip to Antarctica in 1908 with Sir Ernest Shackleton. He was the first person to explore uncharted Antarctic coastlines. The Antarctic base of Mawson is named after him. The picture on the Australian $100 note is from a photograph of Mawson taken by Frank Hurley on the Mawson expedition of 1911. Mawson is wearing:

- a balaclava of hand-knitted wool
- a snow helmet made of **burberry**—a waterproof fabric.

Mawson on the Australian $100 note.

▼ This wedding cap comes from Liptov, a province of Slovakia in Eastern Europe.

▼ A decorated Kohistani child's cap

A decorated cap

This is another example of a cap made by hand. It was made sometime between 1930 and 1940 in Indus Kohistan in northern Pakistan. It was made from black cotton and silk, and red-printed floral cotton. The cap has an embroidered **geometric** design, with white beads, metal coins, and plastic and pearl buttons.

These caps were worn all the time in the cold mountain environment. The shape and decorations protected the wearer from the cold and bad spirits.

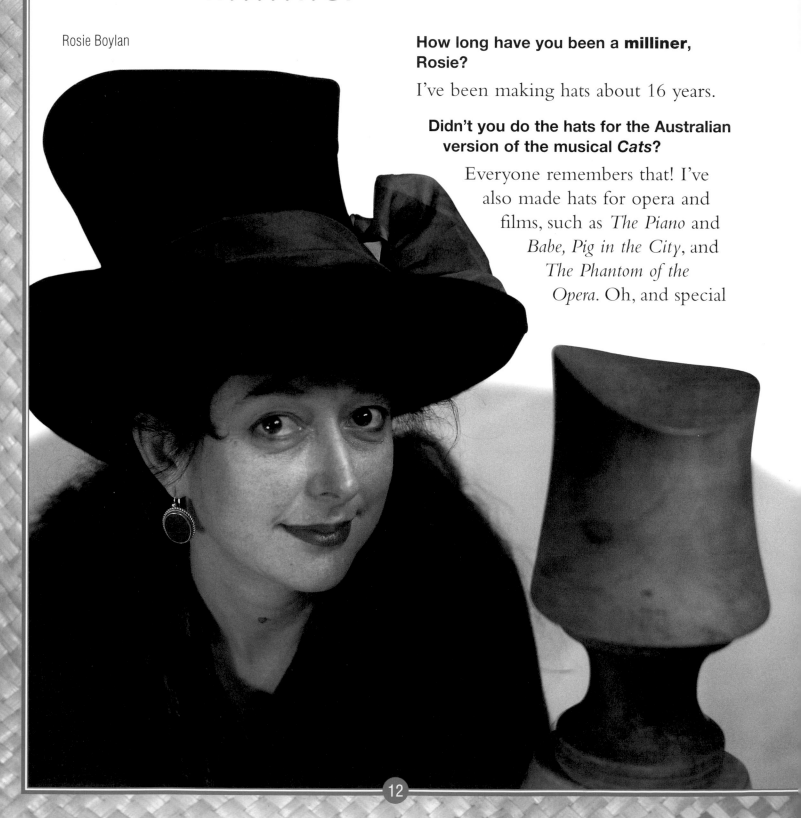

Meet
Rosie Boylan,
milliner

Rosie Boylan

How long have you been a milliner, Rosie?

I've been making hats about 16 years.

Didn't you do the hats for the Australian version of the musical *Cats*?

Everyone remembers that! I've also made hats for opera and films, such as *The Piano* and *Babe, Pig in the City*, and *The Phantom of the Opera*. Oh, and special events such as the parrot headdresses for the closing of the Olympic Games in Atlanta. I've made hats for individual clients. My hats have dined with the Governor, gone to Russia and taken walks beside the Hawkesbury River.

Tell us what is involved in making a hat for someone.

I meet with the client and find out what the hat will be used for. Is it for a special occasion like a wedding? Is it to wear in the garden to keep the sun off? I measure their head circumference above the brow and look at their height, head and body shape, proportion and coloring. I ask them what sort of decoration they might want—things like ribbons, flowers or bows. I think about the 'look' which will suit their personality.

What do you mean by coloring and proportion?

I look at the color of their skin, eyes and hair and think about the colors of the hat which will complement their own colors. A hat with a great big brim would probably not suit the proportions of a short person—they might look like a mushroom…

Oh no!

I then look for materials and start doing the technical work—making the hat. At the next meeting with the client, we fit the hat and see how it suits them. Changing the height of the crown or width of the brim just a little

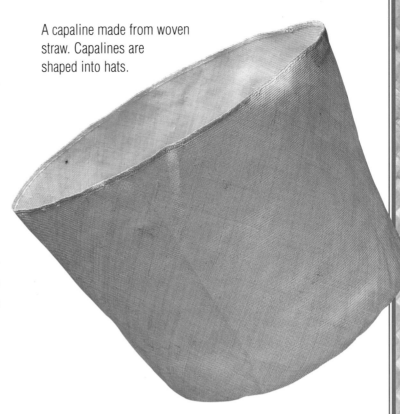

A capaline made from woven straw. Capalines are shaped into hats.

can make a big difference. At the last meeting, the client collects their hat with perhaps some small changes.

What do you use to make a hat?

I use steam to change the shape of materials, needles and thimbles, scissors, hat blocks and natural fibers.

What is the best part of your job?

In theater or film, I like being drawn into the world being created. I like working as part of a team with interesting people to help make the characters fit into this world. I do this by making the hats which are just right for the character. With individual clients, the joy is having gone through a process with them to make a hat which brings their personality alive. They feel the hat is 'right' and so do I.

Make a hat

Pretend you are a milliner and make this hat for a friend.

What you need:

- felt, cardboard or stiff material
- scissors
- craft glue
- accessories such as flowers or cotton for stitching

Step 1

Interview your friend. Ask them what colors they would like, and how they would like their hat decorated.

Step 2

Measure the circumference of your friend's head. This will be the size of the crown.

Step 3

Cut out the brim, side and crown of the hat. Allow for a seam. The circumference of the crown should be at least three centimeters (one inch) bigger than your friend's head and the same length as side D of the crown.

Step 4

Apply glue to the seamline of both the crown and inner edge of the brim at regular intervals.

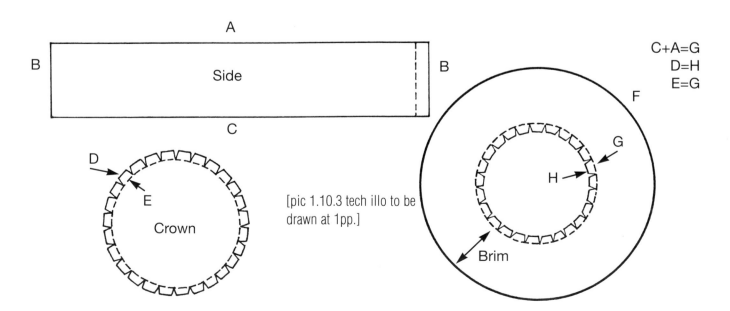

[pic 1.10.3 tech illo to be drawn at 1pp.]

Step 5

Join the edges of the upright cylindrical section.

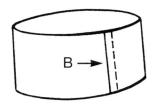

CHALLENGE 1

What do these sayings mean?

- I'll eat my hat.
- At the drop of a hat.
- To pass the hat around.
- A feather in your cap.

The answers are on page 30.

Step 6

Glue the tabs into position to join the crown to the upright section, making sure that the tabs are inside the hat.

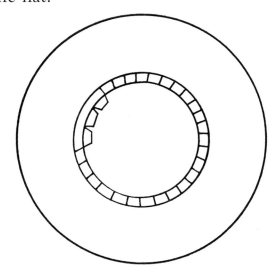

Step 8

Decorate the hat. In the examples shown, the black felt hat is oversewn with a blanket stitch and cross-stitch. There are crêpe-paper flowers on the pink cardboard hat. Or you could appliqué, embroider, or use artificial fruit, beads, braid, feathers or flowers.

Blanket stitch

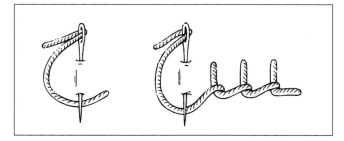

Cross-stitch

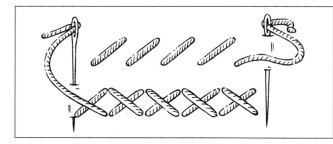

Step 7

Glue the tabs into position to join the brim to the upright section, making sure that the tabs are located inside.

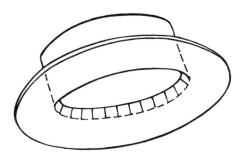

Gloves and mittens

Archaeologists say that hand covers were worn by cave-dwellers hundreds of thousands of years ago. The cave dwellers' mittens were sewn with a needle made of bone. Knitted mittens have been found in Egyptian tombs. In ancient times, gloves were worn for both decoration and to protect the hands of workers. Later, warriors and hunters wore gloves. Gloves were also worn by kings and bishops to represent their power. Gloves are not only made to protect hands—they can be decorative.

▼ A pair of cream net lace mittens with satin drawstring ribbons

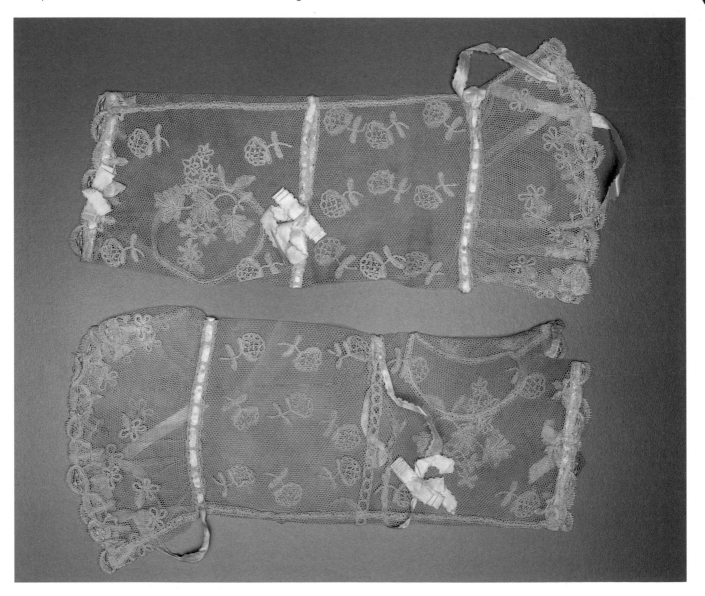

Messy Madeleine has six red woollen gloves and six green woollen gloves all mixed up in her drawer. What is the smallest number of gloves Madeleine has to pull out to be certain of getting a pair?

The answer is on page 30.

▲

Woollen gloves, hand-knitted by Myra Mogg, Australia, around 1940

▶

Spanish or Italian **ecclesiastical** gloves made of knitted silk and silver metallic thread in the 1600s

Glove stories

- Gloves used to be exchanged when buying and selling land.
- Knights wore one of their lady's gloves on their breast as a sign of love.
- Hundreds of years ago, when a young man married, he gave the father of his bride one of his gloves as a sign that he would take care of his daughter.
- Chinese people extend a gloved hand to mean they are pleased to see you. In other cultures, you must remove your glove before offering your hand.

Muffs

Muffs are soft bags that open at both ends. They were used by men, women, boys and girls to warm their hands and to carry things such as hair combs and even small dogs! They were first used in France around 400 years ago. From around 200 years ago, muffs were mostly worn by women and girls, until the early 1900s when they became less fashionable.

This muff is made of **swansdown**. This pure white muff must have been very difficult to keep clean.

This child's muff was made in Australia around 1880. It is red velvet with a red silk corded strap. It has a red velvet bonnet to match.

This muff was made of platypus fur, silk and linen between 1850 and 1900. The platypus has been protected from hunters since 1900.

Minnie and her muff

Minnie Peters is best known as Ginger Meggs's girlfriend in the Ginger Meggs comic series. She is always wearing her muff. Ginger first appeared in 1922, and Minnie soon after.

▲ Minnie Peters doll

► A Victorian child's bonnet and muff made of red velvet

Hand puppets

This is Bunyip Bluegum and Sam Sawnoff, two glove puppets based on characters from *The Magic Pudding* by Norman Lindsay. Both have **papier mâché** heads and cloth glove bodies. Bunyip is a young koala and the hero of the story. Sam is a penguin and the owner of the pudding.

This is Bunyip Bluegum (left) and Sam Sawnoff (right), two glove puppets made in 1945 by William Nicol.

The Nintendo® Power Glove

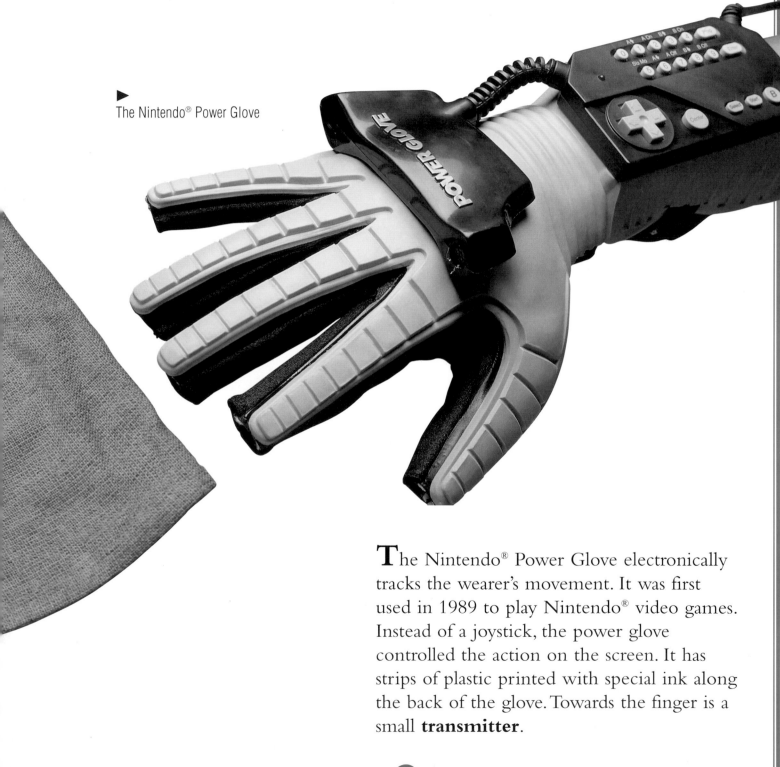

▶
The Nintendo® Power Glove

The Nintendo® Power Glove electronically tracks the wearer's movement. It was first used in 1989 to play Nintendo® video games. Instead of a joystick, the power glove controlled the action on the screen. It has strips of plastic printed with special ink along the back of the glove. Towards the finger is a small **transmitter**.

Types of shoes

'The silver shoes,' said the Good Witch, 'have wonderful powers. And one of the most curious things about them is that they can carry you to any place in the world in three stages, and each stage will be made in the wink of an eye. All you have to do is to knock the heels together three times and command the shoes to carry you wherever you wish to go.'

From *The Wonderful Wizard of Oz*
by L. Frank Baum, 1900

Feet, like hands, are an important part of the body. Our feet need protection. But as with hats and gloves, we wear shoes for other reasons as well. Shoes have a practical purpose but are also an object of beauty.

◄ A man's shoe made of black suede with thick tread synthetic sole, designed by Mambo Graphics, Australia, 1992

◄ A man's boot made of leather, metal, rubber and synthetic, designed by Dirk Bikkembergs, Belgium, 1996

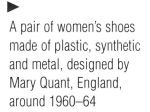

► A pair of women's shoes made of plastic, synthetic and metal, designed by Mary Quant, England, around 1960–64

▲ A pair of men's sandshoes called 'Wunala Dreaming' made of canvas, rubber and cotton, designed by Ros and John Moriarty of Balarinji Design Studio, Australia, 1995

22

Tiger shoes

The shoes pictured below are children's slip-on shoes appliquéd with fabric pieces and embroidered to look like tigers. Made by hand in China some time between 1900 and 1950, these shoes give enjoyment to their owner and also good luck! The tiger is a Chinese symbol of courage and bravery.

▲ A pair of women's shoes called 'Portrait of a Slipper IV', made of kangaroo leather and designed by Donna-May Bolinger, Australia, 1993

▲ Chinese tiger shoes

Lucky shoes

The hidden shoe

The style of the shoe pictured below suggests it was made in the early 1700s. It was found in 1904 hidden in the wall of a house in England. During the 1700s, shoes were used as charms to ward off bad luck.

► The hidden shoe

▼ Ferragamo shoes

Golden shoes

These sandals were made by a famous Italian shoemaker called Salvatore Ferragamo in 1938. He padded the straps and covered the cork platform with hand-painted silk and tiny glass beads. They look very luxurious. However, he made them only out of materials available to him. He said there was 'no end to the materials a shoemaker may use to decorate his creations.'

Musical shoes

There are many songs about shoes. Do you know any of these?
- 'Boots of Spanish Leather' (Bob Dylan)
- 'These Boots are Made for Walking' (Nancy Sinatra)
- 'Blue Suede Shoes' (Elvis Presley)
- 'Put on Your Dancing Shoes' (Cliff Richard)
- 'Old Brown Shoe' (The Beatles)
- 'Sailing Shoes' (Little Feat)
- 'Put my Little Shoes Away' (Everly Bros)
- 'Walk a Mile in my Shoes' (Joe South)
- 'Golf Shoes' (Mental as Anything)
- 'Soul Shoes' (Graham Parker)
- 'Hi Heel Sneakers' (Jose Feliciano)
- 'Who's Gonna Fill Their Shoes?' (George Jones)
- 'Doctor Martin Boots' (Alexei Sayle)
- 'No Shoes' (John Lee Hooker)
- 'My Walkin' Shoes' (The Nitty Gritty Dirt Band)
- 'Goody Two Shoes' (Adam Ant)
- 'Knockin' Boots' (Candyman)
- 'Oh, Dem Golden Slippers' (African American spiritual)
- 'The Cobbler's Song' (Norton–Asche)

Shoe timeline, 1700–1880

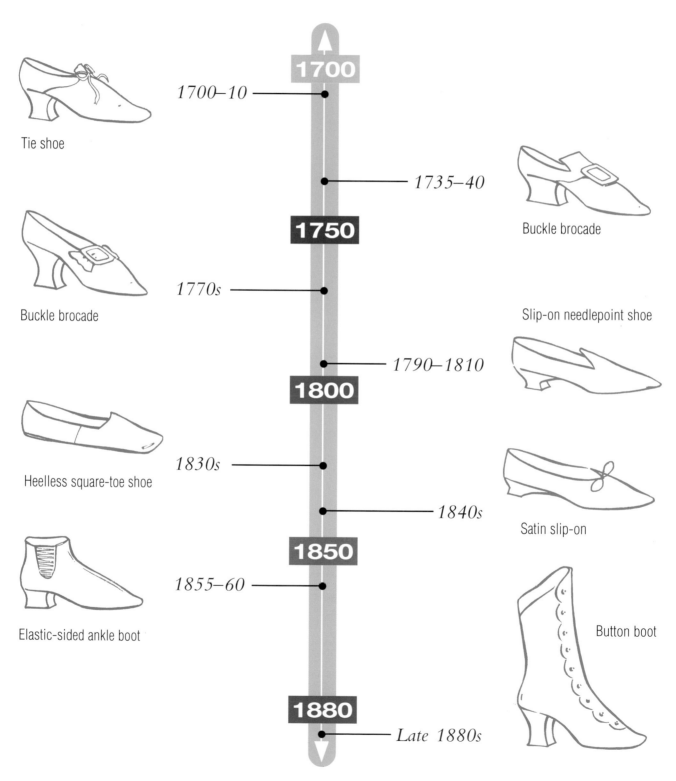

Tie shoe

1700–10

1735–40

1700

1750

Buckle brocade

Buckle brocade

1770s

Slip-on needlepoint shoe

1790–1810

1800

Heelless square-toe shoe

1830s

1840s

Satin slip-on

1850

1855–60

Elastic-sided ankle boot

Button boot

1880

Late 1880s

Parts of a shoe

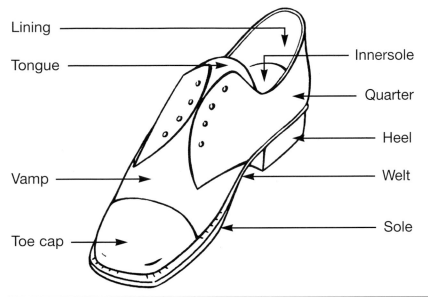

- Lining
- Tongue
- Vamp
- Toe cap
- Innersole
- Quarter
- Heel
- Welt
- Sole

CHALLENGE 3

Compare each of these shoes to the timeline and guess how old they are.

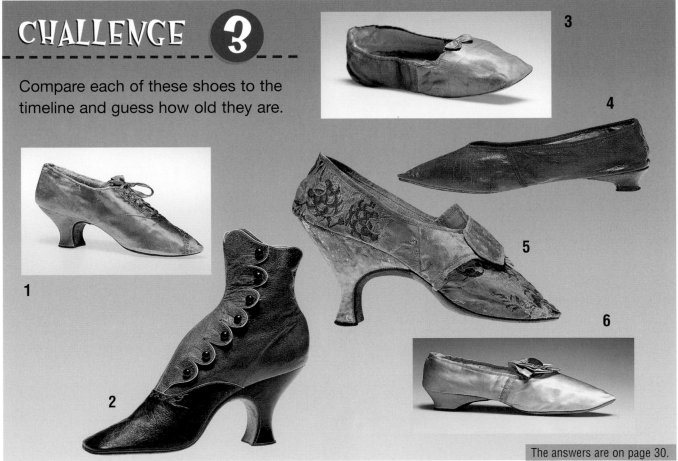

1 2 3 4 5 6

The answers are on page 30.

How a shoe is made by hand

Step 1

The basis for all shoe making is a wooden model of a foot, known as a **last**. It is used to make a paper pattern of the shoe. Two lasts are made—one for each foot.

A last

▲ Shoe designer Donna-May Bolinger in her studio

Step 2

Leather is then cut from the pattern for the upper, lining, sole and innersole of the shoe.

Step 3

The pieces of the upper are joined, along with the calf-skin lining.

Step 4

A 'stiffener' is slipped between the leather and the lining at the quarter. A firm 'toe puff' is used to fix the shape of the toe.

Step 5

All the edges are trimmed.

Step 6

The innersole and upper are fitted to the last, and tacked together.

Strong linen thread is used to replace the tacks and joins the upper to the innersole.

The sole is attached to the shoe.

The heel is attached. It is often made of leather.

Stockings and socks

The socks below do not fall down when you walk. The socks have more elastic woven in the ankle than at the top so that they 'push up' as you walk.

This stocking was made by a 12-year-old girl for an exhibition of women's industries in 1888. It was made of cotton with fancy knitting at the top and foot.

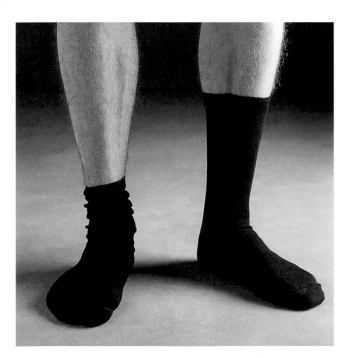

A pair of men's 'Holeproof Computer socks', made of wool and nylon by Holeproof Socks Pty Ltd, Melbourne, 1990

◄ A child's stocking from Holland, 1888

Clothes for heads, hands and feet

This book is full of interesting and delightful examples of clothing that covers heads, hands or feet. These types of clothing are called 'accessories'—things that assist the way we look. However, as you can see, some of the accessories in this book not only assist, they are essential!

Coverings for heads, hands and feet can warm the body, shield it from the sun, and protect it from sharp sticks and stones and harmful chemicals. Throughout history and in some cultures, these coverings had to be worn not only for protection but because the wearers were obeying social rules.

Coverings for heads, hands and feet protect us and say something about us. These coverings decorate our bodies. They show how creative we can be.

Myra Mogg knitted the covering on these shoes in the late 1930s.

CHALLENGE

In this book is another item of clothing made to match these shoes. See if you can find it.

The answer is below.

Answers

Page 15

'I'll eat my hat' means that you do not believe what someone is telling you.

'At the drop of a hat' means that you will do something quickly or perhaps unexpectedly.

'To pass the hat around' means that you are collecting money, probably for a gift.

'A feather in your cap' means that you have received a reward.

Page 17

Madeleine has to pull three gloves out to make sure she gets a pair.

Page 27

Shoe 1 is a brocaded tie shoe with heel from 1700 to 1710.

Shoe 2 is a side button boot from the late 1800s.

Shoe 3 is a heelless square-toe satin slip-on from 1830s.

Shoe 4 is a needlepoint slip-on from 1790 to 1810.

Shoe 5 is buckle brocade shoe from the 1770s.

Shoe 6 is a satin slip-on shoe from the 1840s.

Page 30

Myra Mogg also made the gloves pictured at the top of page 17.

Glossary

agals   hoops of thick cord, wool or goat's hair that hold the 'Kaffiyeh', or cloth of an African head-dress, in place

aigrettes   plumes, or tufts of plumes, made from feathers and used as a European woman's head-dress

balaclavas   knitted caps that pull down over the head and under the chin

burberry   a cloth treated to make it waterproof and used to make overcoats and suits

ecclesiastical a descriptive word meaning something to do with the church

fronds   the divided leaves of plants such as ferns and palms

geometric   a descriptive word for something that has mathematical shapes such as squares and triangles

gourd   the fruit of a climbing plant. The shell of this fruit can be dried and used as a container or a head covering

headset   a device that fits over the head. It is generally used for listening to a radio but can be connected to a computer for images and sound

immersive   to be surrounded by another world

last   a mould or wooden form over which a shoe is built

linen   fabric made from a flax plant

milliner   a person who makes or sells hats

muffs   soft bags that open at both ends, used to keep the hands warm

papier mâché a strong substance made of paper pulp mixed with glue

swansdown   fine soft feathers from a swan

tiaras   pieces of jewelry that look like a crown and are worn on the head

transmitter   a machine for broadcasting or sending a message

Index

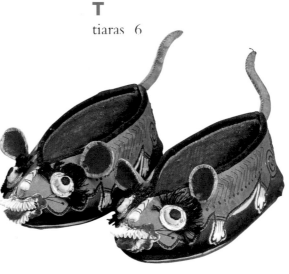

Photo credits

All objects featured in this publication are from the Powerhouse Museum collection, unless otherwise indicated. The Museum acknowledges the many generous donations of objects, which form a significant part of its collection.
★ Indicates photographs of museum objects reproduced with the permission of the designer or maker. Photographs are by the Powerhouse Museum, unless otherwise indicated.

Cover: shoes★ by Balarinji Design Studio.
Title page: shoes★ by Balarinji Design Studio.
Page 3 Portrait shoes★ by Donna-May Bolinger; page 4 Funkessentials poster★ by Sara Thorn and Bruce Slorach; page 5 'Mary Don't Ask' ★ by Peter Tully, courtesy Merlene Gibson; page

6 Funkessentials beanie★ by Sara Thorn and Bruce Slorach; Mambo cap★ by Gerry Wedd for Mambo Graphics; Marinara tiara★ by Dinosaur Designs; Ceramic shawl★ by Martin Boyd Pottery; feathered hat★ by Philip Treacy; Hmong headdress, photo by Fong Siu Nang; page 9 Immersive head set, photo courtesy Cybermind UK Ltd; page 10 $100 bill, courtesy Reserve Bank of Australia; page 12 Rosie Boylan; pages 22/23 Mambo shoes★ by Mambo Graphics; Balarinji shoes★ by Balarinji Design Studio; Portrait shoes★ by Donna-May Bolinger; page 24 Ferragamo shoes★ by Ferragamo; page 28 Donna-May Bolinger; page 29 Computer socks★, photo courtesy Holeproof.

Please visit the Powerhouse Museum at **www.phm.gov.au**